RICH OFF INFLUENCE

From Traps to Apps™

Unlocking Exposure Illiteracy

You Were Never Broken

You Were Underexposed

Jeremy Newkirk

From Bay Road to Beverly Hills

Published by BeOfficial MG™ Publishing

First Edition

Printed in the United States of America

This book is an independent work based on the author's personal experiences in the music and media industries. References to artists, record labels, and companies; including the appearance of their logos, are used solely for factual and descriptive purposes to illustrate the author's past professional affiliations. No artist, record label, or company referenced in this book has authorized, sponsored, endorsed, or approved this publication. All trademarks and logos remain the property of their respective owners.

DEDICATION

I dedicate this book first to God, and then to myself. Writing has always been my passion, and publishing a book has been a lifelong dream. I am grateful, proud, and deeply fulfilled to see that dream finally come true.

To my sons, Jeremy A. Newkirk and Jebari N. Newkirk—

My voice of reason since the moment you were conceived in the womb. You are the reason I pledged to stop hustling blindly and start showing up with intention. Words can't express the gratitude I have for fatherhood or the joy and love I gained by raising two strong young men. You have already invested so much into my life just by being present, and only God can repay that value. I love you both deeply.

To my mother Dequilla N. Carr—

My rock and my lifelong cheerleader. The queen who sacrificed everything so I could live the way I do today. A true Proverbs 31 woman. Without you, there would be no me. I love you forever.

To my grandmother, the late Evangelist Bessie Newkirk aka Mrs. Honey —

My prayer partner. My shield. A woman of strength and determination who pushed our entire family into a new way of living and thinking through faith in God. You prayed for me and believed in me long before I learned how to pray and believe in myself. I miss you deeply. Please tell Grandad I love him and thank him for teaching me to never quit and to always be strong. And to all her children and grandchildren I love all yall!

To my step pops Gregg Carr—

Thank you for loving us unconditionally and always being there, no matter what. I love you, King.

To my father Elder Major Newkirk Jr.

I'm grateful to God we always fought through every obstacle to unite in love. I appreciate the practical and spiritual knowledge you pour into me every day. Thank you.

To everybody who grew up on Bay Road.

To all my friends and family in Wallace, Pender, Ivanhoe, Dunn, and Charlotte, NC

To my DC, MD, and VA, family

To my business partners and extended family at BeOfficial Management Group and Cover360ixty

To all my employers who help sustain my life

To everyone in the world who was taught how to hustle and survive but was never taught how to properly own and thrive.

This book is dedicated to you.

START HERE

If this book resonates with you, continue the journey.

Visit Getrichoffinfluence.com for resources and tools that help turn influence into ownership.

Contents

PREFACE

You Were Never Broken

You Were Underexposed

If you are reading this book, there is a high probability that you are intelligent.

Capable.

Hardworking.

And structurally underexposed.

Let me say that clearly:

You were never broken.

You were underexposed.

Underexposed to ownership.

Underexposed to equity.

Underexposed to insulation.

Underexposed to backend control.

Most people do not fail because they lack effort.

They fail because they lack literacy in systems that compound.

You were taught to work.

You were not taught to own.

You were taught to hustle.

You were not taught to insulate.

You were taught to be grateful for opportunity.

You were not taught to analyze contracts.

That gap is not moral.

It is structural.

And structure determines permanence.

This book is not a motivational story.

It is not a rags-to-riches narrative.

It is not about fame.

It is not about flexing success.

It is about translation.

It is about taking intelligence that survived chaos

and repositioning it inside protected architecture.

You may see parts of yourself in Bay Road.

In Ivanhoe.

In the bridge.

In boot camp.

In executive rooms.

But this book is not about me.

It is about the pattern.

The pattern of underexposed brilliance.

The pattern of visible hustle and invisible vulnerability.

The pattern of influence without ownership.

The pattern of participation without position.

For years, I built systems I did not own.

I strengthened infrastructure that did not protect me.

I confused visibility with leverage.

I confused income with permanence.

And the correction cost me time.

Time you may not want to lose.

This book is written for:

The builder who is tired of strengthening rooms they don't control.

The creative who signs contracts they don't fully understand.

The employee who deserves equity literacy.

The parent who refuses to pass ignorance forward.

The entrepreneur who knows they are capable but feels something missing.

What's missing is not ambition.

It's architecture.

You are not behind.

You are underexposed.

And exposure is correctable.

But correction requires confrontation.

You will be challenged in these pages.

Not emotionally.

Structurally.

You will be asked:

Do you own what you build?

Do you understand the math of equity?

Do you know what survives you?

If those questions feel uncomfortable,

good.

Discomfort precedes literacy.

And literacy precedes sovereignty.

This book moves in stages:

Survival.

Confrontation.

Awakening.

Permanence.

It mirrors transformation.

Not perfection.

Nothing in these pages glorifies the trap.

Nothing in these pages romanticizes chaos.

Everything in these pages translates it.

From traps to apps.

From hustle to infrastructure.

From proximity to participation.

From survival to sovereignty.

Read slowly.

Audit yourself honestly.

Complete the Architect's Reflections.

Do not skip the uncomfortable questions.

Because this book is not here to entertain you.

It is here to equip you.

And once you see the system clearly,

you will never again confuse being valuable…

with being powerful.

Now turn the page.

The curriculum begins.

PART I SURVIVAL WAS CURRICULUM

Survival is not weakness.

It is training.

But training without translation becomes a ceiling.

Some of us were not raised with leverage.

We were raised with endurance.

We learned how to stretch food.

Stretch patience.

Stretch faith.

Stretch effort.

We learned how to read rooms before we read contracts.

How to sense danger before we sensed dilution.

How to move quietly before we moved strategically.

We inherited hustle.

We did not inherit infrastructure.

Nobody explained equity.

Nobody explained ownership.

Nobody explained insulation.

We were told:

Work hard.

Stay humble.

Be grateful.

Endure.

And endurance kept us alive.

But endurance alone does not produce sovereignty.

This section is not about glorifying struggle.

It is about decoding it.

Because survival trained your instincts.

It sharpened your perception.

It built resilience into your nervous system.

The problem was never your capability.

The problem was exposure distribution.

Some children grow up hearing about trust funds.

Others grow up hearing about survival funds.

Some children learn how to read balance sheets.

Others learn how to read people.

Both are intelligence.

Only one compounds automatically.

Survival was curriculum.

But it was incomplete.

This part of the book is not here to shame your beginnings.

It is here to reveal them.

To show you what they trained you for.

To show you what they did not prepare you for.

To show you that ceilings feel normal when you've never seen insulation.

Before ownership,

there was endurance.

Before literacy,

there was instinct.

Before sovereignty,

there was survival.

And survival deserves respect.

But survival must not be the destination.

"Every empire has an address where the dream first began."

Bay Road | Wallace, North Carolina

My grandparents' home where my story began. The yellow-highlighted section marks a remodel project I completed after I first gained access to money, before my grandparents passed away.

This house on Bay Road in Wallace, North Carolina represents the foundation of everything that came later. It was my grandparents' home, the place that shaped my early understanding of family, work, and perseverance. After I first gained access to money, one of the first things I did was remodel part of the house before my grandparents passed away. Looking back, it wasn't just a renovation—it was a small sign that success should always reach back and touch the place that raised you.

CHAPTER 1 BAY ROAD

Where Survival Was Curriculum

I'm from a small town called Wallace, North Carolina.

If you blink while driving through it, you'll miss it. That's how small it is. But small doesn't mean simple. And it definitely doesn't mean easy.

I grew up on Bay Road, in a house they call a shotgun house—long, narrow, and crowded. About twenty people lived under one roof, squeezed into maybe 1,200 square feet. Privacy wasn't a concept. Silence wasn't an option. You learned early how to move around people, how to listen, how to wait your turn.

My mother had me when she was still in the 12th grade, just months away from graduating high school. My father had already joined the military. They lived on the same street. After my mom graduated, she followed him to Newport News, Virginia, trying to build something that never quite took shape.

It didn't last.

My father disappeared. My mother came back home—to my grandmother, to her siblings, to Bay Road.

My grandmother was the backbone of that house. She worked at my middle school cafeteria and carried the responsibility of feeding both her family and hundreds of students every day. My mother worked long hours in a sewing factory, stitching stockings, doing repetitive work that never paid enough but demanded everything.

Money was always tight. But structure was everywhere.

Every morning around 4:00 or 4:30 a.m., I woke up and went with my grandmother to the cafeteria. While other kids slept, I learned how meals were planned, how ingredients were measured, how timing mattered.

Nothing happened by accident. You couldn't just throw things together and hope it worked.

Looking back now, that cafeteria was my first operations center.

That's where I learned that preparation determines outcomes. That execution matters more than intention. That finishing the job—every single day—was non-negotiable.

I didn't know it then, but those mornings shaped how I would see the world forever.

Noise, Faith, Escape

Bay Road was never quiet.

Not ever.

My grandmother's house was alive in a way that felt almost unreal when I look back at it now. Loud. Crowded. Always moving. Always full. Imagine a house where teenage mothers and their children lived under one roof—my mother being one of them.

My grandmother had eleven children. Most of them girls. Two boys passed away before I was born. That meant I grew up surrounded almost entirely by women. My mother. Her sisters. Their children. My grandmother herself was only in her late thirties, maybe early forties, already a grandmother to a growing pack of kids.

Think about that for a moment.

A grandmother still young, raising children who were raising children.

The house was packed. Noisy. Chaotic. Full of laughter, arguments, jealousy, love, frustration, and survival. It was everything a child could want—and everything a child could want to escape from.

My grandmother was deeply religious. There was no room for anything the devil could take credit for in that house. Everything was Jesus. Morning, noon, night. Church wasn't optional—it was law. Faith was protection. Discipline was love.

My grandfather wasn't around much. When he was, he carried his own storms. So for most of my early years, it was me, my grandmother, and a house full of women.

And me—one of the only boys.

I didn't know how to name it then, but I always felt out of place. Too much noise. Too much emotion. Too many eyes. I didn't know where to go. Where to run. Where to skate. Where to be alone.

So I escaped where I could.

A few houses down from my grandmother's place, my Uncle Fit had a plum tree in his front yard. That tree became my refuge. I'd sit there eating plums, watching the street, imagining myself leaving Bay Road. I didn't know how. I didn't know when. But I knew I wasn't going to stay forever.

Then my father appeared.

Second grade.

One day I was sitting in Ms. Woodard's class, and a tall, dark-skinned man walked in. He spoke quietly to my teacher. They whispered. Then they pointed at me.

I hadn't seen my father in years.

I didn't know who that man was.

Ms. Woodard called me to the front of the class and asked, "Jeremy, do you know this man?"

I said no.

She said, "This is your father. He's here to pick you up."

Back then, if you were the parent, you didn't need permission.

My father took me home.

I was terrified.

I didn't know him. He introduced me to male cousins I didn't even know lived on the same street. That same day, he bought me a dog.

For the first time in my life, I felt chosen.

When he returned me to my grandmother's house, my mother exploded. She accused him of kidnapping me. She made me give the dog back.

I had already fallen in love with that dog.

I didn't speak to my mother for days.

That following summer changed everything.

Eventually, my mom allowed me to spend the summer with my father in Durham, North Carolina. I was seven going on eight. It felt like rescue.

I escaped Bay Road.

Durham felt like a different world. Quiet mornings. My own room. No constant noise. My dad cut the jury curl out of my hair—the same curl I had been fighting kids over, trying to prove I wasn't weak, wasn't "soft," wasn't what they called me.

That summer, I learned how to swim. How to play tennis. How to ride bikes freely. My father worked as the head janitor at Century Oaks Apartments and later at Northern Telecom. He showed me electricity, static wristbands, and how invisible systems powered everything.

For the first time, my mind felt calm.

I thought he had come to save me.

At the end of the summer, my mom came to pick me up. I thought they were getting back together.

They weren't.

We got on the Greyhound bus and went back to Wallace.

Back to Bay Road.

Back to noise.

Back to limitation.

That was the first time I felt trapped.

Not physically.

Structurally.

"Sometimes the moments that change your life don't look important until years later."

Second Grade Graduation | Willard, North Carolina

This photo was taken around the time my father came back into my life. Just days later, I traveled to Durham, North Carolina to spend the summer with him, a visit that would change my boyhood in ways I didn't yet understand.

This second-grade graduation photo represents a quiet but important moment in my life. Around the time this picture was taken, my father re-entered my life after being absent. Just days later, I went to Durham, North

Carolina to spend the summer with him. At that age, I had no idea that this experience would shift the direction of my childhood and shape the way I would see the world moving forward.

Looking back now, I realize that many of the moments that shape us don't seem significant when they happen. But sometimes a single summer, a single decision, or a single reconnection can influence the course of a young boy's life.

STRUCTURAL DECODE

Survival Is Not Sovereignty

Bay Road didn't lack intelligence.

It lacked exposure.

Exposure to:

- Ownership structures
- Intellectual property
- Equity
- Insulation
- Backend control

We inherited hustle.

We did not inherit infrastructure.

We inherited resilience.

We did not inherit leverage education.

Survival is reactive.

Ownership is intentional.

Survival keeps you alive.

Ownership keeps you sovereign.

The cafeteria taught me operations.

The plum tree taught me imagination.

Durham taught me exposure.

But no one taught me backend literacy.

That gap has a name:

Exposure Illiteracy.

The inability to read systems even when you are intelligent inside them.

I could feel ceilings before I understood contracts.

I could sense limitation before I understood leverage.

That tension would follow me for years.

ARCHITECT'S TRANSFER

Before you judge your environment, analyze it.

Ask:

- •What did your upbringing train you to endure?
- •What systems were operating around you that you didn't understand?
- •Were you taught ownership or just survival?
- •What ceilings felt normal because you had never seen higher?

You were not broken.

You were underexposed.

And underexposure can be corrected.

"Before I knew I would build businesses, I discovered I could create."

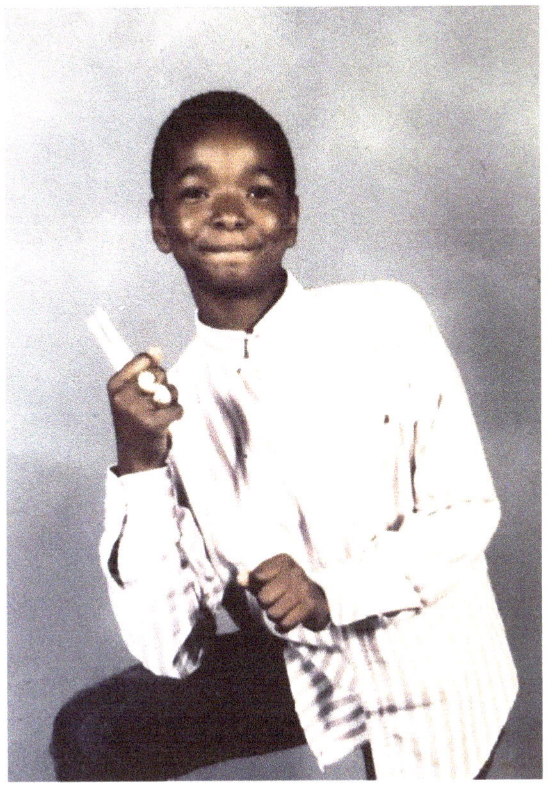

7th Grade | Discovering My Creative Voice

In seventh grade, I wrote my first book and began to realize that I had a creative mind. Around the same time, I discovered my love for music and storytelling—two passions that would later shape much of my journey.

Seventh grade was when I first discovered that creativity lived inside of me. I wrote my first book during that time, and it opened my eyes to something new about myself—I loved creating ideas and turning them into stories. Around the same time, my connection to music began to grow. Music, creativity, and expression became outlets that allowed me to see the world differently.

I didn't realize it then, but those early creative instincts would eventually lead me into the music industry, entrepreneurship, and storytelling on a much larger scale. Looking back now, that seventh-grade moment was the first sign that my journey would involve more than just working for a living—it would involve creating something of my own.

CHAPTER 2 THE FIRST SYSTEMS

Cooking, Code, and Curiosity

I was a quiet kid. Observant. I didn't talk much, but my mind never stopped moving.

Writing became my outlet. I wrote down emotions I didn't have language for yet. Stories. Thoughts. Ideas. Writing gave me control over things I couldn't control in real life.

By the time I reached seventh grade, my habit of waking up early had carried over into school. I'd get to homeroom before anyone else. My teacher noticed. Instead of telling me to sit quietly, she let me turn on the old computers.

This was the era of Oregon Trail. Green text. Black screens. BASIC commands. At first, I just played the games. Then I started paying attention to how they worked. Eventually, I started writing my own simple programs.

That was the moment I realized something important:

Around that same time, my father briefly re-entered my life. He worked in electronics at Northern Telecom. He introduced me to the Commodore 64, to circuits, to electricity, to the idea that invisible forces could be harnessed if you understood the rules.

For a while, it felt like a bridge—something connecting who I was to who I could become.

Then it ended again.

My father remarried. Started another family. And just like before, it was me, my mom, and my grandmother.

But by then, something had already been set in motion.

I wanted to build.

Me and my friends built a log cabin so elaborate the city forced us to tear it down. No permits. No blueprints. We didn't know rules yet—just ambition. When that failed, we tried farming. On land that wasn't even ours.

Failure didn't discourage me. It educated me.

Every attempt taught me something new about coordination, resources, and effort. About what worked—and what didn't.

What I didn't realize at the time was that my curiosity wasn't random.

It was directional.

"Freedom can feel beautiful before you understand the dangers that come with it."

Ivanhoe, North Carolina (Present Day)

At 12 years old, after my mother got married, we moved into what was then a brand-new mobile home in Ivanhoe, North Carolina. For the first time in my life, I had something simple but meaningful—my own room.

In 1988, when I was 12 years old, my life changed again. After my mother got married, we moved into a brand-new mobile home in Ivanhoe, North Carolina. It might not have looked like much to the outside world, but to me it represented something I had never experienced before—space that was mine. For the first time in my life, I had my own room.

That small sense of independence made me feel a new kind of freedom. As a young boy, it felt like a step forward in life. What I didn't understand at the time was that the streets surrounding that new sense of freedom would also introduce dangers and lessons that would shape the man I would eventually become.

Looking back now, that moment represents the calm before many of the storms that would test my character, my judgment, and my future.

CHAPTER 3 THE TRAP IS ORGANIZED

Order Inside Consequence

Ivanhoe didn't feel dangerous.

It felt upgraded.

When my mother married my stepfather and we moved to Trussell Road, I thought we were leveling up. New streets. Different energy. Familiar faces with sharper edges.

Across from us lived my cousin Gee.

He wasn't loud.

He was organized.

Cars came and went.

Money moved efficiently.

People listened when he spoke.

Respect followed him into rooms.

At twelve years old, I didn't see crime.

I saw control.

I saw structure.

There were roles.

Territories.

Schedules.

Hierarchy.

Supply chains.

It wasn't chaos.

It was capitalism without paperwork.

That's what made it seductive.

Bay Road had taught me endurance.

Ivanhoe taught me motion.

The same instincts I used in the cafeteria timing, coordination, execution translated seamlessly.

I watched how inventory moved.

How risk was assessed.

How territory was defended.

How loyalty was enforced.

And I was good at understanding it.

That's the uncomfortable truth.

Underexposed boys don't crave destruction.

They crave significance.

They crave to matter in rooms where power is visible.

And in Ivanhoe, power was visible.

Until it wasn't.

One night cracked the illusion.

Earlier that day, nothing felt unusual. Later that night, someone didn't come home. Conversations shortened. Laughter disappeared. Adults moved differently.

A life was gone.

And with it, the fantasy that power came without consequence.

Courtrooms don't feel dramatic.

They feel sterile.

When the sentence came down life it didn't echo.

It dropped.

Heavy.

Flat.

Final.

Life.

That word rearranges time.

Birthdays erased.

Holidays missed.

Moments that will never happen.

That was the moment I realized:

The system I admired could produce influence.

But not protection.

And a system that cannot protect you is incomplete.

STRUCTURAL DECODE

Street Structure vs Corporate Structure

The streets are not chaotic.

They are organized.

Street Structure includes:

- Immediate cash flow
- Visible authority
- Enforced territory
- Reputation-based leverage
- Loyalty as currency
- Speed over insulation
- It works until enforcement exceeds dominance.
- Corporate Structure also includes:
- Hierarchy
- Supply chains
- Territory
- Performance metrics

But it adds:

- Contracts
- Intellectual property

- Liability shields
- Insurance
- Asset transfer mechanisms
- Legal insulation

Street power depends on presence.

Corporate power survives absence.

Fear protects moments.

Infrastructure protects generations.

The trap is not stupidity.

It is misdirected architecture.

Underexposed intelligence placed inside an unprotected system.

ARCHITECT'S TRANSFER

Ask yourself:

- Does the system you're operating in legally protect you?
- Does it scale without your physical presence?
- Does it compound?
- Does it transfer?

If the answer is no, you are participating not owning.

There is a difference between:

Being effective inside a system

And controlling the system itself.

The trap feels powerful because it rewards competence quickly.

But quick reward without insulation leads to permanent consequence.

The speed of a system does not determine its durability.

And durability determines legacy.

"Some mentors teach you how to succeed. Others teach you what survival looks like."

Gee — My Cousin, My Brother, My First Street Mentor

My big cousin Gee, who I looked at like a brother, was one of my earliest mentors in what I now call "streetology." This photo with my parents marks his 30th year anniversary in prison, serving time from 1989 to 2019. His current projected release date is December 5, 2026.

Growing up, my cousin Gee was more than family to me—he was like a big brother. At a time when I was still trying to understand the world around me, he became one of my first mentors in what I now describe as **streetology**, *the unwritten rules of survival, respect, and reputation that exist in many communities.*

But the streets come with consequences. Gee has spent decades behind bars, beginning in 1989. Seeing someone so close to me lose so many years of freedom left a lasting impact on my understanding of choices, influence, and direction in life.

His story is a reminder that mentorship can shape you in many ways—some that guide you forward and others that show you the cost of certain paths. Moments like this would later influence my determination to transform my experiences into something greater, building a life based on ownership, knowledge, and influence.

CHAPTER 4 CLOSE ENOUGH TO TOUCH IT

The Seduction of Becoming What You See

The streets always collect.

Sometimes they collect money.

Sometimes they collect time.

Sometimes they collect lives.

I watched people I grew up with disappear—some locked away, others lowered into the ground. At first, the funerals shook me. Then they became routine. You stop feeling shock. You start feeling numb.

After prison visits stop feeling frighting…

they start feeling normal.

That's dangerous.

Because once something becomes normal, it stops warning you.

By the time I reached thirteen, I wasn't outside the system anymore.

I was near it.

Close enough to observe.

Close enough to understand.

Close enough to participate.

Proximity changes perception.

When you grow up watching adults work themselves into exhaustion just to survive, organized money feels intelligent.

When you grow up watching respect be withheld, visible influence feels like arrival.

When you grow up under ceilings, movement feels like freedom.

And the streets offered movement.

I wasn't reckless.

I was observant.

I watched who spoke.

Who listened.

Who moved product.

Who collected.

Who enforced.

Hierarchy was clear.

Money flowed daily.

Respect was immediate.

And I understood it faster than I should have.

That was the problem.

Underexposed boys don't crave destruction.

They crave significance.

They crave momentum.

They crave to matter.

And the streets reward competence quickly.

At school, I was an honor student.

Teachers saw promise.

At night, I was organizing movement.

Inventory tracked.

Timing calculated.

Risk assessed.

Cash stacked.

I told myself I was in control.

But control is an illusion when the system owns the consequences.

The tension started quietly.

One voice said:

"This is structured. You understand this."

Another voice said:

"You've already seen how this ends."

The line between observer and participant is thinner than people admit.

Especially when the environment rewards your skillset.

The streets didn't seduce me with chaos.

They seduced me with organization.

And I was good at organizing.

Because fast money silences logic.

It convinces you that consequences are for other people. That your intelligence somehow makes you immune.

That's what makes it dangerous.

STRUCTURAL DECODE

Seduction Is Strategic

The trap is not stupidity.

It is validation.

It tells you:

You're smart.

You're capable.

You're respected.

You matter.

But it attaches that validation to fragility.

Here's the structural pattern:

1. Underexposure creates hunger.

2. Hunger seeks visible systems.

3. Visible systems reward competence.

4. Competence builds identity.

5. Identity attaches to system.

6. System enforces consequence.

The danger isn't lack of intelligence.

It's intelligence applied to unprotected architecture.

Every underexposed young man believes he will be the exception.

Smarter.

Faster.

More disciplined.

But systems don't bend to optimism.

They bend to structure.

And street structure lacks insulation.

It produces power without permanence.

And power without permanence eventually collapses.

ARCHITECT'S TRANSFER

Examine your proximity.

- What environments validate you?
- What systems reward your competence quickly?
- Do those systems protect you legally?
- Do they scale without you?
- Do they compound or just circulate?

Ask a harder question:

If the system disappeared tomorrow, what would you own?

Skill is transferable.

Identity is attachable.

Be careful what system you allow your identity to attach to.

Because once identity attaches,

leaving feels like erasing yourself.

And that is where most people stay too long.

This chapter matters because it shows:

You weren't reckless.

You were capable.

You weren't chaotic.

You were structured — in the wrong system.

That nuance makes this book different.

CHAPTER 5 WHO AM I BECOMING?

Performance Under Pressure

Living two lives doesn't explode at first.

It stretches.

Thin.

During the day, I was the version adults approved of.

Clean clothes.

Good grades.

Honor roll.

Business class making perfect sense.

Teachers said I had "potential."

At night, I was something else.

Money moved.

Reputation built.

Presence hardened.

Voice lowered.

Eyes sharper.

Two worlds.

Two reputations.

One body trying to manage both.

At first, it felt like adaptability.

I could shift language.

Shift posture.

Shift tone.

Shift energy.

In school, I was disciplined.

In the streets, I was decisive.

At home, I was respectful.

Outside, I was relentless.

But pressure builds when identity splits.

Because eventually, one world demands proof of loyalty.

The boys tested constantly.

Ball games weren't games.

They were auditions.

Trash talk wasn't noise.

It was ranking.

You either held space

or lost it.

And I held space.

Because invisibility felt worse than risk.

The money stacked faster.

The respect came quicker.

The validation hit harder.

I told myself I was smarter than the system.

I wasn't reckless.

I was strategic.

But strategy without insulation is just delayed consequence.

Arrests started happening.

Nothing catastrophic.

Just enough to warn me.

I ignored it.

Because fast validation is addictive.

Because ego doesn't calculate expiration dates.

Then came the day I ran my sports car I had purchased at just 16 years old into a concrete bridge while driving fast counting money on my way to pick up more money.

Not metaphorical.

Physical.

The car split in half.

Me barely escaping death.

Standing traumatized looking over the river of water that almost took my life.

Breathing heavy.

Realizing something I couldn't ignore:

I wasn't even seventeen yet.

And I wasn't going to live much longer.

That was the first moment fear pierced ego.

Not fear of jail.

Fear of extinction.

The pressure had reached its peak.

Two lives cannot coexist forever.

Eventually, one demands dominance.

And I had to choose.

STRUCTURAL DECODE

Identity Under Load

Dual identity feels like strength.

It is actually fragmentation.

Here's the pattern:

1. Environment rewards adaptation.
2. Adaptation becomes performance.
3. Performance becomes identity.
4. Identity attaches to validation.
5. Validation overrides logic.
6. Pressure escalates.

When identity attaches to external approval,

leaving the environment feels like self-erasure.

That is why people stay.

Not because they are ignorant.

Because they are invested.

You don't just walk away from income.

You walk away from who you think you are.

The bridge moment wasn't about fear.

It was about clarity.

The system I was performing inside

did not have a retirement plan.

It had an expiration date.

And expiration was approaching.

Pressure is not punishment.

It is revelation.

Pressure exposes misalignment.

And misalignment eventually demands correction.

ARCHITECT'S TRANSFER

Ask yourself:

- Where are you performing instead of becoming?
- What identity are you protecting that no longer protects you?
- Is your confidence rooted in ownership or validation?
- If pressure increased tomorrow, would your system hold?

Dual lives create temporary advantage.

Integrated identity creates long-term leverage.

If your environment requires you to fragment who you are,

it is not designed for your sovereignty.

Pressure is not your enemy.

It is your signal.

And when the signal becomes loud enough,

you either pivot

or you collapse.

2014 | A Moment of Realization

In 2014, I had the opportunity to introduce my mother to her favorite actress and one of my mentors, Ms. Debbi Morgan. In that moment, I realized something deeper about the system I was working within.

In 2014, I experienced a moment that was both personal and revealing. I was able to introduce my mother to her favorite actress, the legendary **Debbi Morgan**, who had also become one of my mentors along the way. Watching my mother meet someone she admired so much was a powerful moment of pride for me.

But while standing in that moment, something became very clear to me.

I had worked hard enough to be in rooms with successful people, talented artists, and influential figures. I had relationships, credibility, and experience. Yet I also realized that I was still operating within systems that I didn't truly own.

That realization hit me deeply. It wasn't enough to simply be part of the industry anymore. I wanted to build and control the platforms, systems, and opportunities that shaped it.

In that moment, I knew that my next chapter would not just be about participating in success—it would be about **owning the infrastructure that creates it.**

PART II CONFRONTATION

Every system eventually audits you.

The streets audit with violence.

The military audits with standards.

The market audits with contracts.

Confrontation is not cruelty.

It is exposure.

There comes a moment when instinct is no longer enough.

When charisma no longer compensates.

When talent no longer protects.

When reputation no longer insulates.

That moment feels like collapse.

It is correction.

Confrontation strips illusion.

It reveals fragility.

It exposes deficiency.

And deficiency is not shame.

It is information.

Some people avoid confrontation.

They retreat into validation.

They stay where applause is louder than accountability.

But systems that matter do not reward performance.

They reward structure.

You can survive chaos for years.

You cannot bluff architecture forever.

This section of the book is about the reckoning.

The moment you realize:

You are capable — but not insulated.

Respected — but not protected.

Smart — but not structurally literate.

Confrontation feels like loss.

But loss is often the first honest teacher.

If you survive confrontation without ego,

you gain clarity.

And clarity changes direction.

"Sometimes the only way to save your life is to change your environment."

1994 Navy Boot Camp | Searching for a Way Out

By summer 1993 at 16 years old, life in the streets had spiraled so far out of control that I felt the United States Navy might be my only chance at salvation and a new direction.

By 1993, the life I had been living had reached a point where things felt completely out of control. The streets that once felt like opportunity and reputation had started to look more like a trap. Violence, pressure, and constant danger surrounded everyday life, and I began to realize that if something didn't change, the outcome of my story could end the same way it had for so many others around me.

For the first time, I seriously considered leaving everything I knew behind. Joining the Navy started to feel like more than a career path—it felt like salvation. It represented structure, discipline, and most importantly, distance from the environment that had nearly swallowed me.

Looking back now, that moment was the beginning of a mindset shift. It was the first time I truly understood that sometimes the bravest move a young man can make is choosing to walk away from the life that everyone else expects him to live.

"No matter how big the room gets, stay ten toes down in who you are."

Grand Hustle | Lessons in Loyalty and Leadership

Being connected to the ***Grand Hustle family*** *taught me how to stay ten toes down, move with confidence inside major systems, and never lose sight of who I am.*

Being connected to the ***Grand Hustle family*** *was more than just an industry relationship—it was a lesson in character, loyalty, and resilience. Watching how people within that circle navigated the music industry taught me something deeper than business strategy.*

It taught me how to stay ***ten toes down****.*

In an industry where people often change who they are to fit into different rooms, the real power comes from remaining authentic and confident in your identity. The Grand Hustle culture showed me how to move inside a massive machine like the music industry without losing your foundation.

*That lesson stayed with me. No matter how large the platform became or how many doors opened, the key was always the same—****never switch up on who you are.***

CHAPTER 6 THE EXIT

Running Toward Discipline

Salvation doesn't always arrive the way you expect.

Mine showed up in the form of a Navy recruiter.

The Navy recruiter didn't promise freedom.

He offered a mirror.

He pulled me aside one day at school. Said he'd heard good things about me—and bad ones too.

I told him the truth. I loved electronics. I loved business. But I also told him about my environment. About survival. About doing what I had to do.

He didn't smile.

He said something simple:

"You're fighting a serious battle. You can stay here and become nothing or you can leave and build something."

I didn't hear patriotism.

I heard confrontation.

He wasn't attacking my intelligence.

He was questioning my direction.

By then, I had arrests.

Reputation.

Money.

Respect.

And a shrinking future.

The bridge had already happened.

The fear had already settled.

I knew the expiration date was approaching.

The recruiter didn't save me.

He forced a decision.

June 23rd, 1994.

Great Lakes, Illinois.

Seventeen years old.

Boot camp doesn't ease you in.

It strips you down.

Hair gone.

Clothes gone.

Name replaced with a number.

Voice drowned by commands.

Nobody cared about Bay Road.

Nobody cared about Ivanhoe.

Nobody cared about reputation.

The military didn't negotiate with ego.

It dismantled it.

When they asked who had leadership experience, I raised my hand.

JROTC.

Drill team.

Rifle team.

They put me in charge of marching the company.

A hundred men.

Some older.

Some bigger.

Some louder.

My heart pounded.

But fear was familiar.

I called cadence.

Forward march.

They followed.

Not because I was aggressive.

Because I was clear.

Within weeks, I became Recruit Chief Petty Officer.

We were on track to be a color company highest honor in training.

Then education caught me.

A reading comprehension score flagged.

ASMO'd.

Removed from leadership.

No warning.

No appeal.

No negotiation.

The system didn't care about potential.

It cared about standards and according to the US Navy I was not as smart as I thought I was.

That hurt more than arrest ever did.

Because jail had never stripped my future.

Education almost did.

That day, I made a vow:

Ignorance would never disqualify me again.

Boot camp wasn't escape.

It was confrontation with vulnerability.

I went back into training. Quiet. Focused. Humbled.

That second company still became a color company.

Different role.

Same impact.

Boot camp stripped away my ego.

Leadership taught me who I really was.

And loss showed me the cost of not owning every part of myself.

STRUCTURAL DECODE

Discipline Exposes Weakness

Street structure rewards dominance.

Military structure rewards discipline.

Dominance reacts.

Discipline anticipates.

Dominance is loud.

Discipline is consistent.

Consistency compounds.

The confrontation wasn't with authority.

It was with deficiency.

Talent without literacy is unstable.

Instinct without education is vulnerable.

Leadership without comprehension is temporary.

The ASMO moment exposed something deeper:

I had been operating on instinct my entire life.

And instinct had limits.

The streets taught me survival.

Boot camp taught me structure.

But structure without knowledge still collapses under scrutiny.

This was the first time I saw the difference between:

Being capable

and

Being qualified.

Confrontation produces clarity.

And clarity produces correction.

ARCHITECT'S TRANSFER

Ask yourself:

- Where are you relying on instinct instead of mastery?
- What deficiency could quietly disqualify you?
- If your system audited you today, what would fail?

Discipline reveals gaps.

It does not create them.

When a system removes you, don't react with ego.

Respond with elevation.

Education is insulation.

Standards are not punishment.

They are protection.

If you want root access,

you must survive audit.

And audit begins with confrontation.

CHAPTER 7 ESCAPE VELOCITY

Why Distance Isn't Freedom

The military gave me something the streets never could.

Distance.

Distance from temptation.

Distance from noise.

Distance from people who knew the old version of me too well.

On my ship, I read constantly. Books became anchors. Writing became therapy. For the first time in my life, I could think without watching my back.

I traveled. I learned. I followed orders and, for the most part, stayed out of trouble.

I told myself I was done.

But distance without transformation is just a pause.

I hadn't rebuilt my identity yet. I had only removed myself from the environment that challenged it. And the truth is—if you don't replace who you were, the old version eventually finds you.

I didn't know it then, but escape velocity isn't about how far you go.

It's about how much of yourself you leave behind.

CHAPTER 8 TEMPTATION RETURNS

Philadelphia, Money, and Betrayal

My ship docked in Chester, Pennsylvania.

Because we were in dry dock, we were placed in apartments in Philadelphia.

That geography wasn't accidental. It was fate testing my resolve.

One of my closest friends—someone I had known since the streets of North Carolina—had returned to Philadelphia after high school. He took what I taught him and scaled it. Bigger operation. Cleaner structure. More money than I had ever seen.

The first night I arrived in Philly, we were involved in a gunfight at a gas station.

That was my welcome.

I told myself I was done with that life. I stayed away. Hung out with his brother instead. Tried to be normal.

Then something happened.

His mother's boyfriend put his hands on her.

I stepped in. I stopped it. I protected her.

In the streets, moments like that reset loyalty.

I was family again.

My friend looked at me one day and said something that cut deeper than any bullet:

I was frustrated. Racism in the ranks. Pay issues. Promotions delayed. I felt boxed in again—this time by respectability instead of survival.

And here was fast money. Organized money. Familiar money.

I stepped back in.

I told myself it was temporary. Just until I stacked enough to walk away clean.

But there's no such thing as clean money in a dirty system.

Things got hot fast.

Then someone I trusted snitched.

The operation collapsed overnight.

I ran.

I ended up in Connecticut, hiding out—but even on the run, I did what I always did.

I organized.

I built another operation. Marijuana this time. Different product. Same instincts.

That's when it hit me:

This wasn't about drugs.

It was about compulsion.

Starting things.

Scaling things.

Controlling systems.

My gift had been pointing me toward something bigger.

But I kept using it in the smallest possible way.

My mother called me constantly.

"Turn yourself in."

"They're coming to my house."

I could hear fear in her voice.

Not disappointment.

Fear.

So I stopped running.

I turned myself in.

CHAPTER 9 ZERO POINT

Washington, D.C. and Starting From Nothing

When I walked out, I wasn't a hustler anymore.

I wasn't a sailor either.

I came to Washington, D.C. with a white Acura Legend, a Rolex, a fifteen-thousand-dollar chain, about ten thousand dollars in cash—and no plan.

For the first time in my life, movement stopped.

No momentum.

No identity.

No safety net.

Just silence.

I had to confront the truth:

Everything I'd ever built before had been powered by urgency.

Now I needed intention

An aunt gave me an opportunity to do sound engineering at a church. Not glamorous. Not fast money. But structured.

I learned discipline again—this time without fear.

Then something unexpected happened.

I found family I didn't really know.

An aunt who was a computer scientist at IBM.

An uncle who was a GIS scientist for the U.S. Army.

They didn't judge me.

They taught me.

We talked systems. Computers. Logic. Why things worked.

I went back to school.

Business first.

Then computer science.

Slowly. Methodically.

By twenty-five, I had built companies again—tech, real estate, construction. Projects turned into deals. Deals turned into numbers.

But I made the same mistake again.

I didn't own the intellectual property.

I built platforms and watched others walk away with the real power. I was labeled an employee while others became owners.

That lesson hurt worse than jail.

Because this time, I had done everything "right."

Then life hit again.

Marriage. Divorce.

The 2008 real estate collapse.

Property lost. Stability gone.

And then I became a father.

That changed everything.

I refused to disappear.

I took over a nonprofit and renamed it Go Virtual Green. I worked with schools. Kids. Communities. Teaching technology, creativity, and systems.

That's when the truth finally settled in:

My past wasn't a mistake.

It was training.

The streets taught me demand.

The military taught me discipline.

Technology taught me scale.

I just needed ownership.

Zero point wasn't the end.

It was the reset.

CHAPTER 10 OWNERSHIP IS POWER

The Most Expensive Lesson

For a long time, I thought I was winning.

I was building companies.

Launching platforms.

Moving in rooms most people only saw on television.

From the outside, it looked like success.

From the inside, it was something else entirely.

I had learned how to build—but not how to own.

I created platforms that generated traffic, attention, and revenue. I brought talent together. I structured operations. I solved problems that other people didn't even know how to identify.

And then the paperwork came.

Titles like event coordinator.

Consultant.

Contractor.

Labels that sounded respectable but meant one thing:

I didn't own anything.

I didn't understand intellectual property at the level I needed to. Trademarks. Copyrights. Patents. Licensing. Equity structures. I was executing at a high level—and getting paid like an employee.

I watched people walk away with millions from systems I had architected.

That realization cut deeper than any arrest or loss before it.

Because this time, I had done everything "right."

And still lost.

That's when I understood the difference between being valuable and being powerful.

Value gets you paid once.

Ownership pays you repeatedly

Influence without ownership is unpaid labor.

That lesson reshaped everything.

"Respect the culture—but understand the business."

A Lesson from Fat Joe

Through a mutual friend and Grand Hustle family member, the rap artist ***5ive Mics****, I had the opportunity to meet hip-hop royalty* ***Fat Joe****, who shared a powerful piece of wisdom with me about navigating the music business.*

One of the most valuable things about being around successful people is the wisdom they share in simple moments. Through a mutual friend and Grand Hustle family member, the rap artist **5ive Mics**, I had the chance to meet **Fat Joe**, one of hip-hop's most respected figures.

During that conversation, he gave me a piece of advice that stuck with me.

He said, *"There's consciousness, and then there's the bag. You gotta know how to separate the two—because business is business."*

That statement carried a lot of meaning. In creative industries like music, emotions, loyalty, and culture are always present. But the business side operates differently. Decisions about money, ownership, and opportunity require clarity and discipline.

That lesson reminded me that understanding the balance between **principle and profit** is essential if you want to survive—and thrive—inside large systems.

CHAPTER 11 SYSTEMS, NOT SYMPTOMS

Where Structure Became Visible

The military gave me discipline.

Technology gave me vision.

Before tech, I could feel structure.

Inside tech, I could see it.

Servers humming behind locked doors.

Networks layered in silence.

Permissions granted and denied without emotion.

Protocols running whether anyone noticed or not.

It was the first time I understood power without performance.

You don't see the server room.

But it controls the building.

You don't see backend architecture.

But it determines user experience.

Frontend is influence.

Backend is control.

That realization hit me slowly.

On the ship, I read constantly. Manuals. Technical documentation. Books about systems. Books about business. Books about strategy.

I wasn't just consuming information.

I was decoding patterns.

Electricity.

Circuits.

Infrastructure.

Redundancy.

Failover systems.

Access levels.

Everything had insulation.

Everything had hierarchy.

Everything had protection layers.

Nothing critical operated exposed.

And that's when it hit me:

The streets had structure.

But no insulation.

Bay Road had discipline.

But no backend literacy.

I had spent my life inside systems.

But never inside protected ones.

Technology made something visible that had been invisible my entire life.

You can't bluff infrastructure.

It either works.

Or it doesn't.

There is no ego in a failed system.

Only correction.

That clarity felt like awakening.

Not motivation.

Recognition.

I had been solving symptoms.

Now I could see architecture.

STRUCTURAL DECODE

Backend Control Changes Everything

Every system has layers.

User level:

You can operate.

You can participate.

You can perform tasks.

Admin level:

You can configure.

You can modify.

You can optimize.

Root level:

You control permissions.

You control architecture.

You control deployment.

You control protection.

Most people are trained for user access.

Very few are taught how to pursue root access.

That was the pattern I saw everywhere.

In music:

Artists negotiate visibility.

Labels negotiate ownership.

In business:

Employees negotiate salary.

Investors negotiate equity.

In culture:

Influencers build audience.

Platforms own infrastructure.

Frontend performs.

Backend compounds.

Symptoms are visible.

Systems are hidden.

And until you understand backend control,

you will keep solving surface problems inside someone else's architecture.

The awakening wasn't about technology.

It was about leverage.

ARCHITECT'S TRANSFER

Examine your position.

- Are you operating at user level?
- Are you optimizing someone else's system?
- Or are you studying architecture?

Ask deeper:

Who owns the server?

Who owns the contract?

Who controls permissions?

Who has root access?

If you don't understand the backend,

you will misdiagnose your ceiling.

Don't chase visibility.

Study infrastructure.

Because backend control determines permanence.

And permanence determines sovereignty.

CHAPTER 11 ROOT ACCESS

The Thing I Was Really Searching For

Technology gave me a language I didn't know I'd been looking for.

User access.

Admin access.

Root access.

Most people never think about access levels.

They just log in.

They operate inside permissions already defined for them.

They click.

They execute.

They perform.

But they cannot change the system.

That distinction altered everything.

User level:

You can navigate.

Admin level:

You can adjust.

Root level:

You control architecture.

Permissions.

Security.

Deployment.

Ownership.

Root doesn't ask permission.

Root defines it.

And that's when something clicked inside me.

All my life, I had been close to power.

Close to influence.

Close to movement.

Close to visibility.

But not inside it.

The streets showed me front-end dominance.

The military showed me disciplined execution.

Technology revealed backend control.

The pattern was undeniable.

Front-end performs.

Back-end compounds.

I wasn't chasing money.

I was chasing root access.

I didn't want applause.

I wanted authority over structure.

The difference is permanent.

STRUCTURAL DECODE

Proximity Is Not Participation

Most underexposed communities are trained for performance.

Very few are trained for ownership.

Here's the structural trap:

You can build the room.

Design the stage.

Organize the talent.

Drive the traffic.

And still not own the building.

Proximity creates the illusion of power.

Participation in ownership creates actual power.

You can sit at the table.

And still not control the contract.

You can generate revenue.

And still not control equity.

You can create culture.

And still not own intellectual property.

Root access requires:

- Legal literacy
- Equity awareness
- Contract fluency
- Asset protection understanding
- Insulation strategy

Without root access, influence is rented.

And rented power expires.

This was the confrontation:

I had been strong.

But not sovereign.

Capable.

But not insulated.

Respected.

But not protected.

And protection determines permanence.

ARCHITECT'S TRANSFER

Ask yourself directly:

- Do I own what I build?
- Do I control permissions?
- Do I hold equity?
- If this scales, who benefits most?
- If I disappear, does my leverage remain?

If your answer is unclear, you are operating at user level.

That is not shame.

It is awareness.

But awareness demands elevation.

Stop asking:

"How do I get in the room?"

Start asking:

"Who owns the room?"

Stop asking:

"How do I get paid?"

Start asking:

"What percentage do I control?"

Root access is not about ego.

It is about insulation.

And insulation is the difference between survival and sovereignty.

"From Bay Road to building homes; proof that knowledge can change your address."

Bowie, Maryland | 2002–2003

The second home I built from the ground up at just 25 years old—funded through wealth I created in technology and real estate.

At just 25 years old, I made a decision that would shape how I looked at money for the rest of my life—I chose ownership. Between 2002 and 2003, I built this home from the ground up in Bowie, Maryland. The resources that made it possible didn't come from luck or inheritance. They came from the opportunities I created through technology and real estate.

For me, this house represented more than property. It was proof that knowledge, discipline, and vision could change the direction of your life. A young man who grew up on Bay Road had learned that wealth wasn't just about earning income—it was about building assets that gave you control over your future.

Looking back now, moments like this were the early foundations of what I would later call **Rich Off Influence**.

PART III THE AWAKENING

Awakening is not inspiration.

It is recognition.

It is the moment you see the system clearly.

Not emotionally.

Structurally.

You begin to understand:

Frontend performs.

Backend compounds.

Visibility is rented.

Ownership is permanent.

Access is temporary.

Equity is positional.

This is where most people feel anger.

Because literacy reveals what ignorance concealed.

You realize how many rooms you built but did not own.

How many deals you entered but did not control.

How many systems you strengthened without insulation.

Awakening is disruptive.

It rearranges how you negotiate.

It recalibrates your ambition.

It changes your questions.

You stop asking:

"How do I get in?"

And start asking:

"Who owns this?"

You stop asking:

"How much does this pay?"

And start asking:

"What percentage do I control?"

This section is not about wealth.

It is about literacy.

Because literacy changes posture.

And posture changes outcomes.

Awakening is uncomfortable.

But it is irreversible.

Once you see architecture,

you cannot return to surface thinking.

CHAPTER 12 EXPOSURE ILLITERACY

The Silent Ceiling

You were never incapable.

You were underexposed.

Let's confront it.

Most people reading this are intelligent.

Hardworking.

Resilient.

Talented.

And structurally illiterate.

Not book illiterate.

System illiterate.

I was.

I could read Scripture.

Read rooms.

Read risk.

Read opportunity.

But I couldn't read ownership.

I didn't understand cap tables.

Licensing agreements.

Equity dilution.

Asset separation.

Intellectual property strategy.

Insulation layers.

And nobody around me did either.

That's not stupidity.

That's exposure distribution.

Exposure is not evenly allocated.

Some children grow up hearing words like:

Trust.

Equity.

Shares.

Ownership.

Contracts.

Others grow up hearing:

Hustle.

Respect.

Survival.

Grind.

Both require intelligence.

Only one compounds.

Exposure Illiteracy is the inability to read protected systems even while operating inside them.

It is the reason:

- Artists sign bad deals.
- Builders lose equity.
- Founders lose control.
- Employees never accumulate leverage.
- Creators build platforms they don’t own.

It is not laziness.

It is structural absence.

And it is expensive.

STRUCTURAL DECODE

The Pattern of Underexposure

Here's how it works:

You are taught effort.

But not leverage.

You are taught performance.

But not ownership.

You are taught income.

But not equity.

You are taught opportunity.

But not contract language.

So you enter rooms excited.

You build.

You execute.

You add value.

And someone else compounds.

Because they understand backend control.

This is not conspiracy.

It is literacy.

In music:

Artists negotiate visibility.

Labels negotiate ownership.

In business:

Employees negotiate salary.

Investors negotiate equity.

In culture:

Influencers generate traffic.

Platforms own infrastructure.

The front-end performs.

The back-end compounds.

Exposure Illiteracy convinces you proximity equals power.

It does not.

Participation in ownership equals power.

And once you see that distinction,

you cannot unsee it.

That is the disruption.

ARCHITECT'S TRANSFER

Answer these without ego:

- Do I understand how equity works?
- Do I know how to read a contract fully?
- Do I understand intellectual property ownership?
- Do I separate personal and business liability?
- Do I know what happens if my project scales?

If the answer is no

you are not behind.

You are underexposed.

But underexposure is curable.

Ignorance is not shame.

Refusal to learn is.

Stop glorifying hustle.

Start studying structure.

Stop chasing rooms.

Start analyzing ownership.

Because once literacy enters your life,

negotiation posture changes permanently.

And the ceiling you thought was permanent

becomes optional.

CHAPTER 13 FROM TRAPS TO APPS

Translation, Not Escape

Traps to Apps is not a slogan.

It is translation.

It is the reapplication of misdirected intelligence into protected systems.

Nothing about the streets lacked intelligence.

Nothing about Bay Road lacked resilience.

Nothing about my past lacked capability.

It lacked insulation.

The same mind that tracked inventory on the corner

can track equity in a boardroom.

The same discipline that protected territory

can protect intellectual property.

The same awareness that read danger in a room

can read leverage in a contract.

The difference is not talent.

The difference is structure.

Traps are not chaos.

They are organized systems without legal protection.

Apps are not just technology.

They are scalable, insulated architecture.

Traps generate income.

Apps generate assets.

Traps reward presence.

Apps reward ownership.

Traps create motion.

Apps create compounding.

This is not about abandoning where you came from.

It is about translating it.

CHAPTER 14 OWNERSHIP IS DIFFERENT

The Mathematics of Permanence

For a long time, I thought income meant success.

Money was moving.

Rooms were opening.

Titles sounded respectable.

Coordinator.

Consultant.

Contractor.

From the outside, it looked like elevation.

From the inside, I was renting my brilliance.

I had learned how to build.

I had not learned how to own.

I could assemble teams.

Launch platforms.

Generate attention.

Engineer operations.

But when paperwork arrived, the truth was clear.

No equity.

No intellectual property.

No backend control.

Value was leaving through contracts I hadn't fully understood.

That realization hurt more than arrest ever did.

Because this time, I had done everything "right."

And still lost leverage.

That's when I understood something critical:

Income is movement.

Ownership is position.

Income stops when you stop.

Ownership compounds when you don't.

And compounding is ruthless.

STRUCTURAL DECODE

The Math Most People Ignore

Let's break it down cleanly.

Income:

- Linear
- Time-bound
- Taxed immediately
- Dependent on effort
- Stops with absence

Ownership:

- Equity-based
- Appreciates over time
- Often taxed at capital gains
- Transfers

• Exists independent of daily labor

You can earn six figures.

And still build nothing.

You can generate millions in revenue.

And own zero percent of the asset.

Contracts decide power.

If it is not written,

it is not protected.

Equity determines direction.

If you don't have voting rights,

you don't have control.

Intellectual property determines longevity.

If you don't own the IP,

you don't own the future revenue stream.

Asset protection determines insulation.

If personal and business liabilities mix,

collapse spreads.

Recurring revenue determines durability.

Subscriptions.

Licensing.

Royalties.

Equity distributions.

These are not buzzwords.

They are insulation mechanisms.

Here's the confrontation:

Most people negotiate pay.

Very few negotiate position.

Pay feeds lifestyle.

Position feeds legacy.

That's the mathematical difference.

ARCHITECT'S TRANSFER

Before entering any opportunity, ask:

- Do I have equity?
- Do I understand dilution?
- Who owns the IP?
- Do I have voting rights?
- Is there exit value?
- What happens if this scales?

If your compensation depends entirely on your presence,

you are building income — not leverage.

If your absence does not reduce your ownership,

you are building assets.

Ownership is quiet.

But it changes rooms permanently.

It changes how long you're invited to stay.

It changes what you're allowed to negotiate.

It changes whether your children inherit effort —

or position.

The math is simple.

But simplicity doesn't mean softness.

Income is survival.

Ownership is sovereignty.

Choose accordingly.

STRUCTURAL DECODE

The Movement Blueprint

The movement begins with awareness.

Phase 1 Identify the Trap

Ask:

- Does this system protect me legally?
- Does it scale without me physically present?
- Does it compound?
- Does it transfer?

If the answer is no, you are inside a trap even if it pays well.

Phase 2 Extract the Skill

Everything you survived taught you something:

- Negotiation
- Risk assessment
- Supply chain thinking
- Territory awareness
- Loyalty building

Do not discard the skill.

Reposition it.

Phase 3 Study Protected Systems

Learn:

- Equity
- Intellectual property
- Licensing
- Asset protection
- Recurring revenue

Not casually.

Intentionally.

Phase 4 Seek Root Access

Stop chasing seats at tables.

Study ownership.

Who holds equity?

Who owns backend infrastructure?

Who controls exit value?

Phase 5 Build With Insulation

Register properly.

Protect legally.

Structure contracts intentionally.

Retain equity.

Separate assets.

Phase 6 — Scale With Systems

Automate.

Document.

Delegate.

Design recurring revenue.

Phase 7 Pass Exposure Forward

Teach literacy.

Share frameworks.

Buy copies.

Distribute access.

This is not self-help.

This is structural correction.

ARCHITECT'S TRANSFER

This is where it becomes personal.

Where are you currently operating?

Trap?

Or app?

Income?

Or asset?

Presence?

Or protection?

Movement?

Or compounding?

You do not need a new personality.

You need a new architecture.

Your past trained you.

Your awakening refined you.

Now your responsibility is to build.

Because once you see the system clearly,

staying underexposed becomes a choice.

And the movement only works if you pass it forward.

Traps to Apps is not about me.

It is about generational insulation.

From survival…

to sovereignty.

"A deal can make you visible, but ownership is what makes you powerful."

My First Major Deal | Sony Music

My first major deal with Sony Music was a milestone in my career. But it also taught me one of the most powerful lessons of my life about creativity, ownership, and control.

Signing my first major deal with **Sony Music** was a moment that felt like confirmation that all the creativity, hustle, and vision had finally paid off. Being connected to one of the biggest music companies in the world was exciting and validating. It opened doors and placed me in rooms I once only imagined being in.

But with time came clarity.

That experience taught me a powerful lesson that would shape the rest of my life: **creativity without ownership is still a job**, no matter how impressive the title sounds or how big the platform appears. When you don't own the systems around your creativity, you can contribute to something great and still walk away without the true long-term value.

That realization planted the seed for a new mindset—one focused not just on influence, but on **ownership, infrastructure, and building platforms that I controlled.**

Looking back now, that lesson would eventually become one of the core principles behind **Rich Off Influence**.

CHAPTER 15 THE MOST EXPENSIVE LESSON

Building What You Don't Own

For a long time, I thought I was winning.

I was building companies.

Launching platforms.

Structuring operations.

Solving problems other people didn't even know how to identify.

Rooms were opening.

Executives were listening.

Deals were forming.

From the outside, it looked like ascension.

From the inside, I was renting my genius.

I was the architect in rooms I did not control.

I created systems that generated traffic.

Structured teams that delivered results.

Engineered operations that scaled.

But when paperwork arrived, reality followed it.

Titles sounded respectable:

Event Coordinator.

Consultant.

Strategic Partner.

Contractor.

But structurally, they meant one thing:

No equity.

No ownership.

No backend control.

I strengthened systems that did not protect me.

I built infrastructure inside someone else's architecture.

And when those systems scaled,

the wealth compounded just not to me.

That realization cut deeper than arrest ever did.

Because this time, there was no excuse.

No ignorance.

No chaos.

No confusion.

Just literacy arriving too late.

STRUCTURAL DECODE

Value vs. Power

There is a difference between being valuable and being powerful.

Value gets you paid.

Power determines who gets paid repeatedly.

Here's the pattern I had to confront:

You build something.

It works.

It scales.

Revenue increases.

Visibility grows.

Then ownership is examined.

And if your name isn't on the equity,

your leverage ends at performance.

Execution without equity compounds someone else's wealth.

Skill without insulation creates temporary income.

Ownership without visibility can still compound.

But visibility without ownership evaporates.

This is the most expensive lesson in entrepreneurship:

Being the architect does not automatically make you the owner.

The contract decides that.

Not effort.

Not influence.

Not contribution.

The contract.

That's the sobering truth.

And most people never read deeply enough to see it.

ARCHITECT'S TRANSFER

Examine your current position:

- Are you building assets or building for assets?
- Is your name on the equity or just the email thread?
- Do you understand dilution clauses?
- Who controls intellectual property?
- What happens if the company exits?

If you disappear tomorrow, what remains yours?

This question is uncomfortable.

But necessary.

Do not confuse access with authority.

Do not confuse applause with equity.

Do not confuse visibility with control.

Building what you don't own is not failure.

Staying unaware that you don't own it is.

Literacy corrects vulnerability.

Ownership corrects leverage.

And leverage determines permanence.

PART IV PERMANENCE

Influence fades.

Ownership remains.

Permanence is not loud.

It is layered.

It is insured.

Separated.

Documented.

Transferred.

It is built quietly.

The final shift is not about making more money.

It is about making decisions that outlive you.

It is about understanding:

Income feeds today.

Ownership feeds tomorrow.

Insulation protects both.

Permanence requires restraint.

Restraint in contracts.

Restraint in partnerships.

Restraint in ego.

It requires clarity about what you control and what you don't.

It requires responsibility.

Not just for yourself.

But for those who inherit your structure.

The goal was never escape.

It was translation.

From traps to apps.

From hustle to infrastructure.

From proximity to participation.

From survival to sovereignty.

Permanence is the quietest flex in the room.

And sovereignty does not perform.

It positions.

CHAPTER 16 RESPONSIBILITY CHANGES

THE MATH

Fatherhood Rewrote the Equation

Becoming a father didn't make me sentimental.

It made me precise.

When you're alone, risk feels personal.

When you have children, risk becomes generational.

Before fatherhood, mistakes cost me.

After fatherhood, mistakes could cost them.

That recalibration was immediate.

I had spent my life watching men disappear.

Physically.

Emotionally.

Structurally.

I refused to become a story my children had to explain.

Fatherhood isn't just presence.

It's protection.

And protection isn't loud.

It's planned.

I began thinking differently.

Not in months.

In decades.

Insurance policies.

Asset separation.

Education planning.

Intellectual property ownership.

Equity structures.

Legacy stopped being poetic.

It became logistical.

My grandfather protected with force.

My grandmother protected with faith.

I had to protect with structure.

That was the shift.

STRUCTURAL DECODE

Legacy Is Infrastructure

Legacy is not storytelling.

It is system design.

Here's the equation fatherhood forced me to confront:

If income stops with me,

my children inherit effort.

If ownership survives me,

my children inherit position.

Presence matters.

But permanence matters more.

Fear protects moments.

Conviction protects character.

Infrastructure protects generations.

Most people think legacy is inspiration.

It isn't.

It's documentation.

Ownership.

Protection.

Transferability.

Without:

• Trust structures

• Asset separation

• Insurance layers

• Equity planning

• Intellectual property control

Legacy becomes memory not leverage.

Responsibility changes your negotiation posture.

You stop asking:

“How do I win?”

And start asking:

“What survives me?”

That is a different level of math.

ARCHITECT'S TRANSFER

If you have children or plan to:

Ask yourself:

- Do I own assets that outlive my labor?
- Are my business and personal liabilities separated?
- Do I understand estate transfer?
- Have I built systems that scale without my presence?
- Am I modeling literacy or just effort?

If you don't have children yet:

You are still building someone's inheritance.

The question is whose.

Responsibility doesn't slow ambition.

It sharpens it.

It removes ego.

It removes impulse.

It replaces urgency with architecture.

Because survival feeds today.

Ownership feeds tomorrow.

And tomorrow is not optional when someone calls you father.

"Some trips change your location. Others change your destiny."

Hollywood, California | Capitol Records

The trip to Los Angeles that sealed my fate as an executive and owner of ***Cover360ixty™*** *took place at Capitol Records in Hollywood, California alongside Turbo the Great and Bryce Harris, co-founder of Cover360ixty.*

There are moments in life when everything you have been building suddenly feels real. For me, that moment happened in **Los Angeles at Capitol Records in Hollywood, California**.

Standing there with **Turbo the Great** and **Bryce Harris**, my partner and co-founder of **Cover360ixty**, I could see the vision coming together. What started as mentorship, creativity, and relationships was now evolving into something structured and powerful.

Being in those rooms reminded me of the journey that brought me there—from Bay Road, to the streets, to the music industry, and now into executive leadership. But the biggest realization wasn't about simply being present in those spaces—it was about building a platform that would allow others to reach them too.

That trip to Los Angeles confirmed something inside me: I was no longer just navigating someone else's system. I was building my own.

And that system was **Cover360ixty™**.

"Real ownership begins when you start building systems that empower the next generation."

2017 | The Birth of Cover360ixty

In 2017, I met two young creatives whose ambition pushed my vision for ownership to another level. That moment led to the birth of ***Cover360ixty****, alongside Bryce Harris and Turbo the Great*

In 2017, I met two young talents whose hunger and creativity reminded me of the same ambition I once carried when I was coming up. They were driven, fearless, and determined to leave their mark on the culture.

One was **Bryce Harris**, younger brother of multi-platinum rapper **Tip "T.I." Harris**, founder of Grand Hustle. The other was **Turbo the Great**, who would later rise to become a **Billboard Top 100 record producer**.

Working with them pushed my thinking about ownership to another level. I realized that influence alone wasn't enough—we needed a system that could nurture creativity, protect ownership, and give emerging talent the tools to build their own platforms.

From that vision, **Cover360ixty was born**.

What started as mentorship quickly evolved into something much bigger, a framework for empowering creators, entrepreneurs, and innovators to build influence while maintaining ownership of their ideas.

Looking back now, that moment marked the beginning of a new chapter in my journey: not just building opportunities for myself, but architecting systems that could empower others to do the same.

"Ownership turns a dream into a legacy"

ROC Nation | A Dream Realized

Seeing the rise of billionaire founder and CEO Jay-Z showed me what true ownership and power could look like. From the streets of New York to building one of the most powerful label systems in music history, ROC Nation.

Throughout my journey in music and entrepreneurship, I always looked at **Jay-Z** as one of the clearest examples of what ownership could become. His rise from one of the toughest environments in New York City to building **ROC Nation**, one of the most powerful label and entertainment systems in music history, represented something bigger than success.

It represented control.

Watching that blueprint showed me that influence alone wasn't the goal—**ownership of the system was the real power**.

For years, I carried a vision that one day I would be operating in those same spaces, working alongside executives and artists who were shaping the culture and the business of music.

The day I stepped inside **ROC Nation** and began working with executives and artists there, that vision became real. In that moment, I realized something important: sometimes the dreams you carry quietly for years are actually preparing you for the rooms you're meant to enter.

CHAPTER 17 EXECUTIVE ROOMS ONLY

Arrival Without Apology

I didn't kick the door in.

I walked through it.

There's a difference.

Executive rooms are quiet.

Power doesn't perform there.

It positions.

Conversations are measured.

Voices controlled.

Movements intentional.

Nobody is trying to prove anything.

They're deciding.

What gets funded.

What gets built.

What gets protected.

What gets dissolved.

The first time I entered rooms like that, I didn't feel intimidated.

I felt familiar.

Because I understood systems now.

Not surface systems.

Backend architecture.

I wasn't there to impress.

I was there to evaluate.

That shift changes posture.

From Bay Road to boardrooms,

nothing about my origin disqualified me.

Underexposure did.

And once literacy replaced underexposure,

rooms stopped feeling exclusive.

They felt navigable.

I had spent years close to power.

Music rooms.

Industry rooms.

Cultural rooms.

But proximity is not participation.

Ownership changes the rules of entry.

Now I wasn't asking to be in rooms.

I was negotiating terms inside them.

That's different.

And it's quiet.

STRUCTURAL DECODE

Sovereignty Without Noise

Sovereignty is not dominance.

It is control without performance.

Here's what changes when ownership enters your life:

You stop chasing access.

You analyze leverage.

You stop negotiating pay.

You negotiate equity.

You stop asking for visibility.

You secure position.

You stop reacting emotionally.

You move structurally.

Executive rooms reward:

Preparation.

Clarity.

Contract fluency.

Ownership literacy.

They do not reward volume.

They reward insulation.

And insulation is built long before you enter the room.

The triumphant part isn't arrival.

It's integration.

I didn't erase Bay Road.

I translated it.

The discipline of boot camp.

The structure of technology.

The lessons of loss.

The math of fatherhood.

Everything became architecture training.

Nothing was wasted.

ARCHITECT'S TRANSFER

Executive rooms are not geographic.

They are structural.

You enter them the moment:

- You understand contracts.
- You control equity.
- You protect intellectual property.
- You separate liability.
- You negotiate from position, not need.

You don't need a new accent.

You need literacy.

You don't need louder confidence.

You need backend control.

You don't need proximity to power.

You need ownership of structure.

Rich Off Influence is not fame.

It is sovereignty.

From survival…

to structure.

From structure…

to insulation.

From insulation…

to permanence.

And permanence is the quietest flex in the room.

Big systems don't just test your talent, they test your identity.

Inside the Machine | Lessons from the Music Industry

Navigating inside a massive system like the music industry can either elevate you or erase you.

Working inside a massive machine like the music industry will either make you or break you. It's a system filled with opportunity, talent, ambition, and power—but it's also a system that can easily consume people who enter it without understanding how it truly works.

Over time, I began to see the industry in a way that reminded me of something like ***Beast Games****. Everyone is competing, everyone is trying to survive the next round, and everyone is hoping they make it to the next level. But not everyone walks away the same way they entered.*

Some people come out stronger, wiser, and more in control of their destiny. Others leave stripped of their identity, their ownership, and sometimes even their confidence—lost in the very system they hoped would elevate them.

That realization reinforced a lesson I had already started learning: success inside someone else's machine can feel powerful, but **true freedom only comes when you build or control your own system.**

EPILOGUE NOTHING WAS WASTED

Architecture in Disguise

When I look back now, nothing was random.

Not Bay Road.

Not the noise.

Not the plum tree.

Not the Greyhound bus.

Not the gunshots.

Not the courtroom.

Not the bridge.

Not the uniform.

Not the loss.

Not the contracts I signed too quickly.

Not the equity I didn't own.

Not the collapse.

Not fatherhood.

Not the executive rooms.

Every season was architecture training.

I just didn't have the language yet.

Bay Road taught endurance.

Ivanhoe taught organization.

The streets taught demand.

Boot camp taught discipline.

Technology taught backend control.

Loss taught literacy.

Fatherhood taught permanence.

Executive rooms taught position.

Nothing was wasted.

Even the mistakes were curriculum.

Even the humiliation was instruction.

Even the absence was exposure.

STRUCTURAL CLARITY

The Correction

Survival is admirable.

But survival is reactive.

Sovereignty is intentional.

And sovereignty requires literacy.

If I could compress everything into one correction, it would be this:

You were never incapable.

You were underexposed.

Underexposed to contracts.

Underexposed to equity.

Underexposed to insulation.

Underexposed to compounding.

Underexposed to backend control.

Once exposure enters your life,

ignorance becomes a choice.

That is not judgment.

That is responsibility.

THE MOVEMENT CALL

PASS THE EXPOSURE FORWARD

Do not read this book alone.

Exposure only changes generations when it spreads.

Buy copies for:

- The young builder who thinks hustle is enough.
- The creative who signs deals without reading ownership clauses.
- The employee who deserves equity literacy.
- The father trying to break cycles.
- The mother building without insulation.
- The visionary who keeps performing in rooms they don't own.

Teach:

Contracts.

Equity.

Asset separation.

Intellectual property.

Recurring revenue.

Compounding.

Do not glorify grind without protection.

Do not celebrate income without insulation.

Do not build platforms you don't control.

Do not mistake applause for leverage.

If you learn and don't teach, the gap survives.

If you build and don't protect, the system harvests.

If you gain access and don't secure equity, you remain replaceable.

This book is not about flexing success.

It is about correcting ignorance.

It is about translating misdirected intelligence into protected architecture.

It is about turning traps into apps.

It is about moving from proximity…

to participation.

From survival…

to sovereignty.

From influence…

to ownership.

FINAL DECLARATION

Build what outlives you.

Protect what you build.

Teach what you learn.

Own what you create.

And never again confuse being valuable…

with being powerful.

Nothing was wasted.

Now build.

THE TRAPS TO APPS FRAMEWORK™

1 Identify the Trap

2 Extract the Skill

3 Study Protected Systems

4 Seek Root Access

5 Build With Insulation

6 Scale With Systems

7 Pass Exposure Forward

JOIN THE MOVEMENT

Rich Off Influence is more than a book. It is a movement about turning survival intelligence into ownership systems.

Continue the movement at BeOfficial Management Group, LLC (BeOfficial.com) Owner of Traps to Apps™, Cover360ixty™, $ix Figure Makeover™ and Go Virtual Green™

ABOUT THE AUTHOR

A public speaker and Icon in the tech, business, education, and entertainment industries Jeremy Newkirk is the visionary founder of BeOfficial Management Group, LLC the parent company of Cover360ixty.com, MTB Consulting, and GoVirtualGreen.org, a 501(c)(3) organization. He is also the creator and Executive Producer of the entrepreneurial TV Show $ix Figure Makeover.

BeOfficial Management Group is dedicated to fostering the growth of startups, joint ventures, technology initiatives, major entertainment projects, and training entrepreneurs through "Science, Technology, Engineering, Art, and Math" (STEAM).

A distinguished social entrepreneur and a member of the Forbes Black Excellence Society, Jeremy oversees billion-dollar tech and business projects. He collaborates with and influences politicians, educators, Emmy and Grammy-winning entertainers, Hollywood executives, Fortune 500 companies, and both U.S. and international governments. Known for his exceptional people skills and meticulous attention to detail, Jeremy is committed to addressing critical global issues. His passions include computer science, business strategy, software development, construction, music and TV productions, and youth STEM education.

Jeremy has collaborated with notable figures and organizations, including the Obama Administration, President Buhari's Administration of Nigeria, The TD Jakes Foundation, Forbes, T.I., LaVar Ball, Vanessa Simmons, Emmy award-winning actress Debbi Morgan, Angela Yee, former NFL star Santana Moss, U.S. senators, governors, mayors, the United Nations, GEICO, Sony Music, Roc Nation, Grand Hustle, For Us By Us (FUBU), Starbucks, AT&T, Microsoft, the Department of Education, the Department of Defense, Department of Energy, Department of State, Department of Transportation, NYU, PGCC, Howard University, Bowie State University, Georgia Tech, YALI, and other Fortune 500 companies, celebrity influencers, and startups.

Mr. Newkirk's mission is to create innovative solutions that combat illiteracy and discrimination through family engagement, social technology, digital media, creative coaching, and workforce development.
In 2021, Jeremy was part of the GEICO IT Squad that won a Webby Award, which is recognized as the leading international award honoring excellence on the Internet. The New York Times has described the Webby's as the highest honor of the Internet of Things (IoT).

Additionally, he is an author, an LSDBE partner with Clark Construction, LLC, and serves on the Foundation Board of Prince George's Community College in Prince George's County, MD.

You were never broken.

You were underexposed.

Build.
Own.

Pass the exposure forward.

Rich Off Influence

www.ingramcontent.com/pod-product-compliance
Ingram Content Group UK Ltd.
Pitfield, Milton Keynes, MK11 3LW, UK
UKHW062302290726
14090UKWH00017B/833

9 798234 021434